ART THERAPY JOURNAL

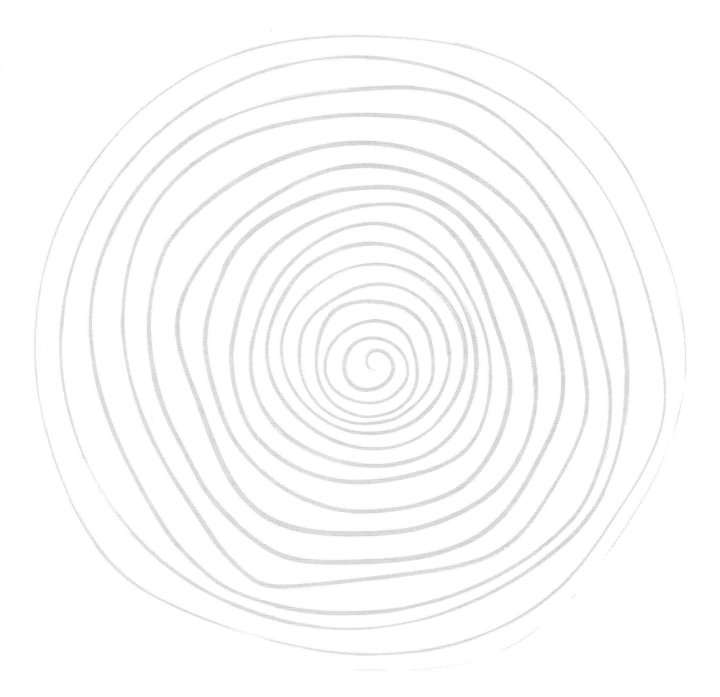

by Emily Bell M.A., LPCC, Art Therapist

© 2023

Welcome

Starting an art therapy journal can be a powerful tool in your self care routine. If you are new to the practice of art therapy, it's definition is simple: engaging in creativity for emotional wellbeing. Many people find art therapy to be a powerful agent for change because of it's mind- body connection; accessing parts of us that words alone cannot express.

The art therapy exercises in this journal are inspired and adapted from the collective wisdom and emergent property of the art therapy profession, ideas of therapists, healers, meditation instructors, poets, artists, Zen Buddhists and most importantly my work as an art therapist.

Any/ all art media are welcome, although you don't need any materials besides a drawing/ writing utensil and this journal to get started. For tutorials and more inspiration join the community on Instagram @ open_mind_therapy_llc. Everyone has an inner artist; let your creativity fly without judgement. No prior art experience is needed.

This journal's goal is for personal expression and not for art critique. If you notice your inner critic while engaging in your Art therapy journaling practice, gently remind yourself: your art is valid and worthy just as it is right now, without needing any technical skill or training. The therapeutic benefits of art can be found in the process of creating it, just as much in the finished product.

Create space for yourself to enjoy the creative process.

Happy Journaling.

MATERIALS LIST

Art prompts can be created using any type of art materials. This list serves as a helpful suggestion.

watercolor paints

oil pastels

colored pencil

colored pens

writing pencil/pen

collage materials/glue stick

MINDFUL ART THERAPY

Mindfulness-based art therapy is a creative practice that encourages you to remain in the present moment. The upcoming pages will guide you through various mindful art therapy exercises.

Much like a meditation routine, engaging in these exercises regularly can help you feel grounded, calm, and at peace.

Mindful art therapy can assist you in recognizing the importance of the creative process. It encourages you to release the need for perfection concerning the final outcome, to remain grounded in the present moment, to release self-judgment, and to fully connect with your body.

Set a timer for 3 minutes, when the timer begins, close your eyes, and hold a writing/drawing utensil as you scribble on the page. See if you can focus on the here and now- what does the utensil feel like in your hand?

What sound does it make?

If your mind starts to wander to what came before or what is coming after this moment, gently bring it back to the sensations and sounds right here in this moment. Let go of any expectations you may have about how the finished product will look when it's done.

Use the next few pages to come back to this anytime you wish to practice mindfulness.

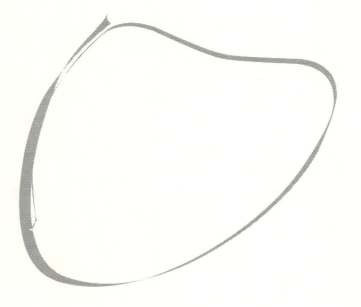

Was it hard to stay present, did your mind wander?
Did 3 minutes feel like a long time? Would you have liked it to last longer?
How did you feel in your body before and after?
Write about your experience:

_____
_____
_____
_____
_____
_____
_____
_____
_____
_____
_____
_____
_____
_____
_____
_____
_____
_____
_____
_____
_____
_____
_____
_____
_____
_____
_____
_____
_____

Fill these pages with scribbles, use both hands at the same time.

Use both hands at the same time, to draw shapes that mirror each other; as if there were a mirror in between your hands.

Set a one minute timer, use both hands at the same time to write your first name, repeatedly, for the entire minute.

Taking a moment to slow down and focus on our breath can help our bodies relax. Pay attention to your breath in its current state; there's no need to alter it. Is it gentle and flowing, or is it fast and sharp? How would you visually represent your breathing? Use lines and shapes to craft an abstract depiction of your breath:

Set a timer for five minutes and let your thoughts flow onto the next few pages through free writing. Write down any ideas or words that come to mind without holding back.

NATURE BASED
ART THERAPY

Nature offers a wealth of metaphors for exploring our identity and life experiences.
In this section, we will draw inspiration from the natural world.
These art therapy exercises can be realistic, abstract, literal, or a blend of all three.
Feel free to express yourself with as much artistic freedom as you desire.

CREATE AN IMAGE OF A MOUNTAIN OR MOUNTAIN RANGE

Suggested material: colored pencils, pen, collage materials, glue

Contemplate unyielding forces, challenging ascents, arduous struggles, concrete thinking, or solid elements. What would you name this mountain?

CREATE AN IMAGE OF NEW GROWTH, SPOUT, OR SEEDLING.
Suggested Material: Colored pencils, watercolor.

In what ways, in what areas of your life do you hope to grow?

CREATE AN IMAGE OF A TREE
Suggested Material: Colored pencils, oil pastels.

Write about your tree, describe its different aspects. What ecosystem does it thrive in?

CREATE AN IMAGE OF A FOREST
Suggested Material: Colored Pencils, Oil pastels,

How does your tree interact with its neighboring trees? In what ways does it receive support? Are the roots interconnected, and what other plants or species coexist in that environment? What is the forest called?

CREATE AN IMAGE OF A NEST.
Suggested Material: Collage materials, glue, oil pastels.

What does your ideal nest look like? Describe your vision of a safe haven where you can relax and find peace.

CREATE AN IMAGE OF A STORM OR INCLEMENT WEATHER.

Suggested material: Watercolors, oil pastels

How do you weather the storms of your life?

CREATE AN IMAGE OF A FLOOD.
Suggested Material: watercolor, colored pencil, pens.

How do you cope with feelings of overwhelm? What resources do you rely on to navigate through challenging times?

CREATE AN IMAGE OF OCEAN WAVES.

Suggested Material: Oil Pastel, watercolor.

Describe your image: Are the waves rough or calm? What ups and downs do you experience in your life?

_____

_____

_____

_____

_____

_____

_____

_____

_____

_____

_____

_____

_____

_____

_____

_____

_____

_____

_____

_____

_____

_____

_____

_____

_____

_____

_____

CREATE AN IMAGE OF WATER AFTER A STORM.

Suggested Material: Watercolor, colored pencil, pen

Give your image a title. What have storms of life left in their wake?

CREATE AN IMAGE OF THE RIVER.

Suggested Material: Watercolor, oil pastel.

Where did it originate? Where are there bumpy, rocky, rapids at times? A detour on the river? Have there been periods of smooth sailing? Sunshine and rainbows? Stormy weather? Unexpected twists and turns?

CREATE A WINTER SCENE

Suggested Material: Oil pastel, watercolor, colored pencil.

During the winter season, creativity, growth, and transformation may seem slow, frozen, or inactive. Reflect on a time in your life that felt akin to winter.

CREATE A SPRING SCENE.

Suggested Material: Oil pastel, watercolor, colored pencil.

In Spring, seeds of growth, ideas, or change may germinate. This may be a
season of new life; dead leaves may turn to soil. Reflect on a chapter in
your life as Spring.

CREATE AN IMAGE OF SUMMER.

Suggested Material: Colored pencil, watercolor, oil pastel.

Summer may be a season of sunshine, powerful storms, full bloom. Ideas, growth, and change may be lush, reaching a peak. Reflect on your image of Summer. Is there a chapter in your life that relates to the summer season.

CREATE AN IMAGE OF FALL.
Suggested Material: watercolor, colored pencil, oil pastel

Fall may be a season of letting go, what is shed can create rich soil
for new growth. Reflect on your image, does it relate to a chapter in your life

CREATE AN IMAGE OF BATTLING ELEMENTS
Suggested Material: Collage Materials, glue, oil pastel.

What keeps you grounded in the midst of inner turmoil? What would you title your image? How would you describe it?

CREATE AN IMAGE THAT REPRESENTS THE SEASON OF LIFE
YOU NOTICE ABOUT YOUR LIFE NOW.

Suggested Material: Watercolor, colored pencil, pen, oil pastel.

What season of life are you in currently? What are the elements you enjoy?
Are there elements that require additional support or tools? What are
some of the challenges of this season?

CREATE AN IMAGE OF A COMPOST OR RECYCLE PILE, ADD ANY WORRIES, CONCERNS, STRESSORS, EXPERIENCES THAT YOU WOULD LIKE TO LET GO.

Suggested Material: Collage Material, glue, watercolor, oil pastel.

Reflect about the items in your compost pile.

FILL THIS PAGE WITH SCRIBBLES SWITCHING BETWEEN YOUR DOMINANT AND NON-DOMINANT HANDS. VISUALIZE LETTING GO AS YOU WORK.

Suggested Material: Pen, colored pencil, oil pastel.

Write about your journey. What is the name of the roads you've traveled? What type of terrains have you navigated?

CREATE AN IMAGE OF A ROAD

Suggested Material: Pen, Colored Pencils.

Reflect about a time you had to make a choice, change course, or were pulled in two different directions.

CREATE AN IMAGE OF A WINDOW, AS IF LOOKING DOWN THE ROAD OR INTO THE FUTURE.

Suggested Supplies: Pen, collage materials, glue.

What do you envision for your future?
What intentions or goals do you aspire to achieve? What qualities or possessions does your future self have that you desire more of?

Write a letter to your future self. What qualities does that future self, have that you need? In what ways does your future self, feel compassion for you self now?

CREATE AN IMAGE OF HURDLES, BARRIERS, OR OBSTACLES.
Suggested Material: Colored pencil, pen, collage materials, glue.

What obstacles stand between you and your future goals? Is there anything that could hinder the connection with your future self. Reflect on any challenges or barriers you may encounter.

CREATE AN IMAGE OF A BONFIRE.

Suggested Material: Collage Material, glue, oil pastel, watercolor, colored pencil, pen.

Is there anything you'd like to put into the fire? Is there anything you would like to take with you?

Write, create, or both about what stands out to you about completing this journal. Are there things you learned about yourself? What ideas you hope to carry forward?

Thank You

Other works by this Author:

Art Therapy Journal for Kids

Mandala a day: Art Therapy Journal

Art Therapy Workbook for Grief & Loss

www.amazon.com/author/openmindtherapy

Join the community on IG
@open_mind_therapy_llc

OPEN MIND
therapy

ACKNOWLEDGMENTS

I want to express my gratitude to the art therapists, both past and present, whose invaluable contributions have influenced the art therapy exercises found in this workbook. This work is a reflection of the collective wisdom, emergent property, and the evolving nature of being part of the art therapy profession. I am thankful for the trailblazing art therapists who paved the way before me, as well as my colleagues whose ongoing efforts enhance my professional skills.

Art Therapy is a clinical approach to mental health, that must be conducted by a trained, credentialed Art Therapist. For more information on art therapy, to find an art therapist, or to explore related research and literature, please visit ArtTherapy.org.